823.92 | HiG | BR

D1513981

Renewals
www.liverpool.gov.uk/libraries
0151 233 3000

Liverpool Libraries

Edgy
Cities

Steve Higginson
Tony Wailey

Published by Northern Lights
P. O. Box 302
Liverpool
L69 8JQ

ISBN 0 9527624 6 3

First published 2006

Designed and Typeset
by The Design Practice
www.thedesignpractice.net
London College of Communication
London

Printed by Crucial Colour
www.crucialcolour.co.uk

ACKNOWLEGEMENTS AND THANKS

For all those who we have lost but not forgotten. (Wild Mint, D.) To the Spider Project which has put so many of us back together and to Julie Tuesday. For those friends at the Liverpool Institute of Popular Music and all the staff @ CaffeLatte.Net, to our 'tide man', Roy 'Boomer' Burns and those who have encouraged us to continue. Finally to Ignazio Corsaro who has published a number of these articles, *Brando, John Lennon,* and *Caravaggio* in the journal *Lo Straniero*.

'Liverpool is an anarchic place where spontaneity and the flamboyant gesture are preferred to the disciplines of tactical thinking and planned interventions. Liverpool is an organiser's graveyard.'
Communist report, 1935.

'I'm gonna wait till the stars come out
to see that twinkle in your eye
I'm gonna wait 'till the midnight hour
that's when my love begins to shine'
Wilson Picket/Steve Cropper
Muscle Shoals Studios, Memphis, 1965.

CONTENTS

Introduction

'I grew up in the sea and the poverty was sumptuous then I lost the sea and found all luxuries grey and poverty unbearable but each time the distant siren of a tug boat came to remind me. Since then I have been waiting. I wait for the homebound ships, the house of the waters the limpidity of the day.' wrote Albert Camus of French North Africa and New York. He could have been writing about Burbo Bank. The sentiments reflect his love of those cities lucky enough to call themselves ports and the way time and being there is constantly 'created' beyond the order of the clock.

These stories are about time and movement and the everyday/night life of port cities. They focus upon Liverpool but they might be about any of the great ports of the world. They form the reason why Liverpool is both a maritime city beloved by tourists and the heritage industry but also a cosmopolitan edgy city whose inhabitants continue to know more of the wider world from the legacy of the maritime economy. Even if that economy effectively died as a mass industry in the 1970s, the culture that was born out of it continues to define the city particularly in movement, and the clusters of time and employment that form around movement. The movement of the boxer, the singer, the guitar player, the D.J., the dancer, itinerant rigger or hotel worker continues to loom alongside a culture – that was born out of the maritime economy. Movement continues to define the city as much as the irregular tides define the river and the city's place on the Atlantic Ocean and the west coast of Europe. A city where the gulf stream meets the Irish Sea and melts into its own illusions like any city of the hurricane ports. Liverpool may be based within a temperate zone but it is not a temperate city.

Theses sojourns illustrate the reason why we should always be concerned with being and time. Although history is supposed to be about time past, to help us shape the present, time can pass history by. You cannot read history backwards. Going back in time is not the time of today. We became aware of how time and place can carry their own illusions after coming across one of the first visual images of 'old' Liverpool. It was one of the first attempts to map England and its composite towns and cities. The historic period being mapped was from 1570, and the New Year began in March. Moving and placing you back in time can be both perceptive and deceptive especially for port cities.

The starting point of the old map depicted London as the capital city and Norwich, the second city of the Kingdom, as the area was the agricultural and manufacturing heartland of England. The map moves on through 'middle' England…

and only after some thought do the dots become joined towards the coastline. Liverpool was mapped on the furthermost tip, on the margin, on the edge. Liverpool has been on the edge ever since. This suits us fine because any port city is related to its physical landscape… a shifting shoreline produces edgy cities and 'edgy' people.

These stories are a series of sojourns, a word that indicates fleeting, of the moment, in Italian casuale. Sojourno also imagines the tempo and rhythm of stepping out into the night and day of a port city, it concerns time and movement the way a dancer considers rhythm. They were first published in an Italian magazine, Lo Straniero, the Stranger based in Naples. It is no coincidence. All cities on the SW Atlantic maritime route, from Liverpool to Naples, New York to New Orleans, Kingston to Boca, have always had more in common with each other and have always been 'strangers' to their own nation states.

Port cities are different. On the one hand, reflecting an intense localism of their own land interior but also having the option of a different plane of experience; a motivated movement out across time and space towards the endless horizon of sky and sea. The ancient description of Liverpool as a 'settlement' betrays the truth. The word itself depicts a settled or satisfied routine. An insult to the true nature of its people; the restless, the dissatisfied, of a turbulent, angry, narky, raging and roaring, a city like its tides 'a city that knows how to celebrate' and a city that is always on the look-out to make you sing and dance. Little wonder Maxim Gorky called the docks and waterfront of Odessa 'my universities'. These are awkward stories about awkward people. Ask any inhabitant of Marseilles, Naples, Algiers, and they will tell you the same.

In these days of 'real-time' communication, our sojourns remember the first World Wide Web; the oceanic tidal currents which shimmy and shake their way around the globe. These cross currents carry with them stories of routes, roots and rootlessness; of those who leave forever; of some that leave and return; and some who don't do either.

These currents and flows gave port cities separate dimensions of time, space and movement; rhythmic qualities which like the shape of the earth is circular and cyclical so everything that goes around comes around. The tides carry the rhythm.

And as so much of today's sciences are concerned with the natural phenomena of time, space, movement, where better to start than in cities of science… our cities of the sea.

Clock

'Alike to him was Time or Tide.' (Sir Walter Scott)

The media have recently reported that the most commonly used word in the English language is 'time'. Although time forms such an important part of our lives, we really do not know much about it. We cannot feel, smell or touch time... all we know is, it is always there; the infernal rhythms of a ticking clock.

In the Middle Ages when the clock was invented, time systems passed from the natural world into the hands of human beings. In Swift's Gulliver's Travels the Lilliputians thought the only God Gulliver worshipped was his watch. Time became idealised. Society, like the clock mechanism itself, was to become exact, measured and uniform. Time control, measurement and obedience became major themes of human history (people are stuck away to do... time). Time became a constant intrusion into everyday life. Time was constructed to be no longer a Stranger.

But no one is born with a modern clock sense. Like all other living organisms, humans have their own unique systems of internal clocks, which determine wide areas of their behaviour. Therefore time is first and foremost a human creation. And even though rulers from Henry VIII and the

American time and motion experts like Frederick Taylor to Lenin and Mao, all introduced new time systems as though they and they alone invented time, the scientific process recognises that time is not God given. People do not pass through time; time passes through them.

Whether Albert Einstein ever lived in a port city we do not know, except that he passed through innumerable women. He came up with the idea that there are no time absolutes; time flows at different rates for different systems and in effect he wished for people to 'imagine as many clocks as they want'. His genius was based on the fact that no time is possible without movement. Einstein produced his theorems at a time of living in a period of new human experience of sight, sound and movement exemplified by moving pictures, the phonograph and the first ever roller coaster at Coney Island, New York. A rush of air and time passing through us.

Taking him up on his offer is to imagine time and movement of the tides as a new dimension of time… Mari-time, based upon the tides and the effects upon those who lived by the sea. In contrast, an example of this 'time construction' would be the six-faced clock which surveyed every part of the river Mersey. Based in the Salisbury half tide dock and constructed in 1848 one year after the moving of Liverpool to Greenwich Mean Time, it symbolised why dockers and seafarers constantly resisted time constraints throughout their history.

The variety of time experiences and influences in maritime culture were always felt differently through the rhythms of the tides. Port cities had a tide sense, never a time sense. Although women and men had been measuring time for aeons, there had been two separate and opposite systems. People on the land were guided by the sun, sunrise to sunset. Without the solar day, the clock could not have been invented. For those at sea, it was the moon that governed due to its gravitational pull on the world's tides. Every day the tide time is different. This worried astronomers as the waxing and waning of the moon and the resultant ebb and flow of the tides made life very 'irregular'.

Port Cities are 'irregular' places. The more irregular their tides the more irregular the cities' culture. The influence of the moon can still be seen today with the words Monday and Month. These important historical pointers always get lost as the debate over time and tides gets highjacked by new age hippies, 'Swampy' hiding in his tree house, or getting dressed up as moon gods and dancing round Stonehenge. To understand the conflict between a solar and lunar day is to realise it concerns authority, power and measured control. This irregularity was why port cities and industry were to become incompatible, especially in relation to labour.

Original time telling used to be such a local affair. Towns, cities and villages all had their own systems. 1884 was the year of the unification of the world's time systems

Greenwich became the world's clock. Trying to reach a unified system only showed the variety of times around the world. Until the late 19th century there were 49 different time systems in the United States alone, notwithstanding the totality of the Americas. Even today there are the 24 world time zones.

The opposition came from areas that were on the edge of these new time zones. A mari-time, the nautical day was noon to noon. At sea, time was counted in nights – not days, that is why in port cities the night time is always the right time. Even after the development of clock-time, port cities still used the tidal clock showing the ebb and flow of irregular tidal patterns. One of the most irregular was for the River Mersey as it was not one but a mix of tides; of the Atlantic, the Irish Sea, and the Gulf Stream. A Mersey melting pot. Well into the 19th century the social shape of Liverpool time was of a tide-table and not the timetable. Imagine, anyone in Liverpool asking a stranger then, 'got the right time on yer mate?' What exactly would the reply have been?

The more people became accustomed to regular time, the more obedient they became. In a seaport where tidal time was erratic and irregular, with no uniform order, the industrial groups to the forefront over issues of time discipline were dockers and seafarers. Control and power over time were to become highly contested areas – mari-time and industrial time, and lasted throughout the 20th century. And whose time was it anyway? Once someone else owns time it becomes a dominance, a control and ultimately a slavery.

Whether at sea or on the docks, delay and waiting time would always be conflictual as both coincide with power and authority systems. Movement always characterises a port city. There is nothing like a delay or queue – in an orderly society – to keep people in their place, patient and patience. This impatience is still echoed in Liverpool and is why the city has proportionately more taxis than London. It is also why the parameters set by 'the big dig' – in reconstructing the downtown area of the city – are reacted against with such fury and to what has now been laughingly changed to 'city of movement'.

Another time vision is the Latin/Spanish culture of time. They do not segment/schedule time. Their time is allowed to breathe… everything becomes an approximation out of which arose *Mañana*, so detested by rationalism and modernity. Going on your holidays in the 1970s to Spain/Ibiza/Tenerife, one of the mysteries was working out when the clubs would open. Then you realised, people socialised only when they were ready and not when the clock dictated. So the clubs would open when the time was right not when time was tight. A similar awareness of casual time is apparent in Liverpool chat, which always ends with 'see you later'; not with some rigid time frame.

And although, time passes and supposedly waits for no

one, the 'impatience' of a port city is also reflected in attitudes towards time itself. As a group of ex-Liverpool seafarers told the Guardian newspaper a couple of years ago, 'none of us could do the clocking on/off, that's why we are all independents'.

This attitude still prevails today in levels of self-employment, some highly erratic and irregular but with all the pitfalls a better option than having time controlled by someone else – even the workers of a major call centre in Speke were deemed to be too flexible by their bosses. Major attempts were made to time discipline Liverpool when it was colonised by the Puritans in the 17th century. Astronomers were concerned not with enriching lives through scientific discovery, but more to seek out the irregular movement of the moon and its link to the tides, in order to seek out the patterning of the Meridians and to bring lines of longitude and latitude under control. Irregularity was subversive. It didn't matter that later the clock face on the Liver buildings would be bigger than Big Ben's, the rhythm of the city was what dictated the pace.

The Puritan enclave in Liverpool had developed clock and watch making miles away from the central market of London, but handy for the time discipline of plantation slavery, a concept framed in Liverpool by the freemason philosopher Francis Bacon MP and his notion of 'the enclosed boundary'. Needless to say, as Liverpool shows today, the attempts to impose time discipline failed miserably.

In terms of irregularity, Einstein's theory of imagining many clocks has shown up in a new science, which originated from the study of living organisms and their environment. What started as fringe experimentation is now a recognised science called Chronobiology. In the late 1950s, science studied organisms living in tidal regions, in particular their biological and physical timing functions.

The discoveries were hugely significant and show the influence as to why port cities make you want to sing and dance; why they have created the musical revolutions of the 20th century; and ultimately whether mari-time is a natural rhythm time.

All of us are born with our own biological clocks. A system of internal clocks, which are a mix of the regular/irregular − the reason they are called circadian is because they last around a day in duration. Can you recognise the mari-time here, the distinct flowers and fauna of the Mersey certainly are aware. Chronobiology identified other living clocks, which had rhythms, and cycles only found in organisms living in a tidal environment, which have direct relevance to human and social behaviour. They are a free range of biological timers solely linked to the tidal pattern; of a lunar night and a lunar year; they coexist and interact with each other separate from and in opposition to the clock and solar day.

The organisms never lose these timers even when removed from their natural habitats; so they are not learned nor imprinted by the environment, but are presents from nature. Huge studies of fiddler crabs on Cape Cod produced these findings. Why does Kirby still hold the same sentiments of Scotland Road and remind you of the Spagga Napoli, bottle strewn San Pedro and the sea-lanes from Brooklyn to Boca on the River Plate?

When all these clocks interact together scientists call it a 'beat phenomena' based on an 'irregular rhythmicity'. In parallel to these experiments, science has identified the wave patterns of the sea as being similar to sound waves of the musical kind. As human beings are also living organisms surely these scientific discoveries can now have some resonance with humans of the world's tidal regions and their homes in port cities in the way music has influenced their daily lives.

Science has proven what has always been suspected; that port cities have natural night/day characteristics of pace, rhythm and tempo markedly different to anywhere else. And the dance and musical revolutions of the 20th century, from New York and the Eastern Seaboard to Liverpool: Mersey beat was the beat of the Mersey. New Orleans and Kingston echo this fact. It was no coincidence. The natural rhythms of mari-time, the beat phenomena, the rhythmicity, is why river cities are rhythm cities.

PARTY ON SISTERS AND BROTHERS.

Place

Questions arise if anyone says we are putting Liverpool on The Map. Where and on what map? In May 1886, the London Illustrated News described Liverpool as 'the New York of Europe; a world city rather than merely a British provincial'.

Liverpool was ever thus. Its people have always known more about Naples/New York than about Norwich/Nottingham more about Baltimore, Boston and Buenos Aires than Bolton, Burnley or Blackburn and latterly Antibes and Malaga more than Accrington or Manchester.

Was Liverpool England or did it have the context of the Atlantic? Whilst English people had a complex genetic inheritance reflecting differing identities for example, Picts, Saxons, Vikings etc, port cities were the products of tidal patterns where remote forces and influences intermingled with the local. And although distant they shared a commonality with each other and not with their respective hinterlands. The locking out of the dockers in Liverpool between 1995 and 1998 produced more support and allegiance from world wide ports than from the English hinterland.

The dramatic context of this hybridity in the origins of

the port city – with other places beyond the nation state – is not the same as the history of agriculture. The name port is derived from the ancient portus, – the implacable enemy of the countryside, serfdom, and the yoke. Coastal land was always historically free land due to the climate and the shallowness of the soil.

The weather and elements always dictated the location of people. Agriculture needs arid central plains; it needs people to be bridled and tied to the soil, sun and master. The road to freedom was always to the coastline – to the edge. The ports were inhabited by groups of women and men who saw agriculture as nothing more than servitude. They were called vagabondi. They made their living moving boats, cargo and wagons. They integrated strangers and foreigners… or anyone who was on the move. Their trade was retail. The ports were free and mobile and not static and servile.

The port of Liverpool was not one of Northern Europe. It faced the ocean. From there retail wheeling and dealing was with the ports on the coastal plains of France, Portugal and Spain. The North Liverpool coastline up to Southport, which today supports a vast amount of vines, trees, flowers and fauna carried over the centuries by the motion, is testimony to the tides and winds of the SW Atlantic. The pine trees of the Gironde can be found at Freshfield and Formby to the coastal north of the city.

The cultural and social context of Liverpool posed a

question: was it of England or the Atlantic? This question always perplexed Henry VIII and Elizabeth Tudor and was the reason why royal edicts constantly placed many prohibitions and restrictions on Liverpool so that it became illegal to trade with the foreigner and stranger.

The shaping by Henry VIII of a new English nation with a new religion – needed to be mapped as a response to the needs of central government. A new visual image of England was needed. Mapmakers had difficulty mapping coastline areas, which were jagged and ragged, as their new religion only accepted the straight and narrow. Latin America bore witness to this throughout the 19th century and witness New Orleans, pre and post Hurricane Katrina.

The plotting of the first map of England followed the points of angles and straight lines clustered on the provincial planes of southern and central England. Liverpool received a far better mapped image from the Spanish preparing their plans for the Armada – their map commented on Liverpool as a 'free land, full of cheap food and wine and full of Catholics'. Some things never change.

Liverpool's location also made it impossible to turn into an idyllic English town. The unique shape of any port is based on the factor of growing inwards and then outwards from the river's edge. In a semi circular fashion the 16th century drawings of Liverpool, Naples, and Marseilles all show identical design. The narrow alleys and streets were interconnected to keep cargoes and people moving. Everything had to be quick. So the inhabitants took on those same qualities; quick minded, witted, making quick money, and with a pace of speech which slows noticeably the further inland you go.

The first map of England produced what it was designed to do; a unitary system of the parochial and the provincial; – the mapping of time and space by 'good queen Bess' – literally miles apart from a world city; which is presumably the point the London Illustrated News was making in 1886.

The question continues, on what map would Liverpool fit? Nowhere is it clearer than in the comparison between the classic English vagabond, so beloved by English Literature and the nomadic seafarer or the distinction between 'home' and 'away', like vagabondi maybe we are all porteños now.

The dashing young English blade – Tom Jones, Jude, Mellors the Gamekeeper in Lady Chatterley's Lover, Wolf Solent – bestrides the English countryside; he is the intellectual wanderer of the provincial wilderness of hills and woods. Yet he only moves from point to point in rigid straight lines within the same time and space. He never crosses boundary lines to seek difference and only keeps returning to the same place, confirming his Englishness and wariness of the stranger.

In contrast the seafarer – brings to life a real geography of time, place and imagination either through the mass desertions which took place in North America and Australia or by jumping ship in Boca, Buenos Aires – to walk around Latin America. On his way no doubt; he would have bumped into Tommy Moore who managed the biggest brothel in Buenos Aires – The Liverpool Light. And maybe once he'd walked around Latin America and had gotten back to Boca Docks he'd take a drink in the Liverpool Bar and the Liverpool House which are still going strong in Puerto Madero. Cross currents continually washed across him, 'the seraphim of the night and of the world city' wrote William Burroughs.

In 1962–63, there was another major attempt to finally put Liverpool on the map. A certain Mr Lennon from Liverpool was waxing lyrically about his city. His words were very descriptive like 'the transient, the complex nature, the irregular and unpredictable, the turbulence which is impossible to stabilise because it comes and goes in the opposite direction to the normal'.

This could have been John Lennon talking about music or Scousers in general. But it wasn't. It was a Mr G.W. Lennon explaining to the Royal Meteorological Society how difficult it was to place Liverpool on a weather map due to the unique nature of its tidal storms and swells.

Move

It is in movement and night that art is best expressed in port cities. The revolutionary art of Caravaggio teaches us that human imagination will always see more in the dark. The irregular motion of the moon always brings out a sense of balance. In 1606, after killing a member of a rival gang, the vagabond artist fled to Naples. The fugitive life always energised him.

He was the most revolutionary painter in the history of art. This outlaw artist is still revered in Naples and Palermo. His art was never constrained and like so much of his life tumultuous and volatile. He painted with an extraordinary amount of pace and movement, speed, (could you get it then?) And spontaneity.

Naples, like any port city always had distinctive rhythms of light, sound and visual imagery conveying a cosmopolitan casual air of time and place; a living and mobile sojourno (society) where horizons were hardly fixed, and always containing the tensions of roots and routes, particularly in the great emigration passages to Buenos Aires, Santos and Barranquilla. A city organised within a maritime frontier.

It is this fluid and liquid modernity that suits port cities. It was what they were built on.

Cities by the sea inhabit spaces of gravity – why people even today gravitate to them, controlled by lunar irregularities. The rhythms of a maritime world were different to the rural, and later the processes of production structured by industry. Casual time became both a preferred model of employment as much as an attitude to life along the waterfront and on the ships. What had originated as an employers' imposition was equally adapted and practised by those upon whom it was visited as a way of life, not just among seamen and dockers, but virtually all workers in Liverpool.

Informal sectors of the economy have always provided alternatives to industrial time discipline. The tyranny of the clock as the instrument of control became the centre of an oppositional culture in port cities. Irregularity, instability and mobility were the common features of waterfront life from Naples to New Orleans, Marseilles – that was called the Liverpool of the South – to Montreal, Liverpool to Boca and New York to New Orleans. The routine was of the discharging of ships within the dock and not the order of the clock. All of these informal ways of living are still greatly misunderstood even today.

Port cities are places of comers and goers, dodgers and drifters, grafters and grifters and anyone who prefers the cool welcoming fugitive night. Caravaggio was never at ease inland. He always preferred the flight and night of the ragged edges of the port city, where the lowest of the low resided. In particular the ragazzi of Naples, always to be found in the gambling dens and brothels and taverns, the nocturnal escapes of the vagabond. Maritime culture has always produced alternate spheres of female activity. Like a ship, a port city has always been labelled as 'She'. Even today Liverpool has a female population that outnumbers men (by 51–49). Very similar to the figures across the American Eastern seaboard from the late 19th century to the present day. The models that Caravaggio used in his art were men and women always from the depths of society.

Caravaggio's sojourns to Naples and Sicily were well known. Naples, the capital of the two Sicilies, considered by medieval commentators as 'a paradise inhabited by devils' and 300 years later by Geraldo Buffalino as 'either a paradise disguised as hell or hell disguised as paradise'. And for its sins, Naples was eternally damned to suffer beneath the angry furies of Mount Vesuvius.

The restless art of Caravaggio draws you into the changing world around him. It cannot be viewed as an isolated phenomenon. His eyes were firmly fixed on the huge sectarian conflict dominating renaissance Europe. This period of history is the most important as it is the only time where turning points in history actually turned. The Protestant Reformation provided an ethos and philosophical template still prevalent today; where continuity has been hidden beneath a false veil of change.

The period was one of huge upheaval. The ideas of the Reformers were to cleanse society of all irregularities. They succeeded on a massive scale. Their ideas were based on achieving the sanctity and purity in a simple, sombre but severe society where everyone was to know their place. The lowest orders could only find salvation in the Kingdom of Heaven through eternal and purifying labour. Purity beliefs and practices were not new. The Reformation was another religious cycle, which needed purity to establish personal and social order. And as in all ancient religions the individual body was always suspect and its movement always to be constrained.

Within the terms of the Reformation for any society to reach an idealised state of purity, then hybrids, fusions and mixes had to be eliminated. Boundaries and limits had to be erected between people, gender, and morals, taste, and even colour. (Think of Henry Ford and the only colour he allowed for his cars was black and then think of the history and the colour blue.) The whole spectrum of life has to become static to attain purity as movement means the threat of crossing over. Even today, the celebration of 'identity' makes static all what Grandmaster Flash called 'the mix'. To celebrate individual identity is to separate. It is here where postmodernism has confused its own project.

Works of art became scrutinised, seeking out hybrid colours, which were deemed to be illusion and luxury and proof of Papist connivance against God. Caravaggio became the firebrand of Catholic palette hybridity. His fusion and mixing of colours deliberately provoked religious reaction. His emotive and provocative use of colour produced his renowned visual chiaroscuro, the varying and mixing of shadow and light; mixing the sensual with the spiritual; the physical with the exotic which later another Naples boy, Martin Scorsese, was later to use in film with his mix of the lower depths of society and Catholic culture in the making of 'Mean Streets'.

The painter Poussin described Caravaggio as 'The artist who came to destroy all art'. The religious war against image and colour continued to be pursued long after Caravaggio's death, eg, the drabness of the still life of Rembrandt.

The drinking, brawling, roaring life of Caravaggio always took him to the Italian port cities of Genoa, Naples and Ribetta. (The Beatles sang of *There's a Place* on their first album.) And like John Lennon later, he always preferred the ocean at his back. But whilst Martin Luther and John Calvin railed against the artificial means of illumination as sacrilege to the divine, and invoked against the dark subliminal order, 'We ought not to turn day into night or night into day', a Neapolitan Priest, Father Rocco, publicly declared Naples as nocturnal domain of the Catholic Church, by erecting lamplit statues of the Madonna along every waterfront street in the city.

Waterfront art is always of the night just as Catholic symbolism has always been constant in maritime culture. The Virgin Mary was the goddess of port cities and the protector of seafarers. She was the first maritime navigational guide – the starry night, the pole star; she was the Star of The Sea, the Stella Maris. The sanctuary of The Stella Maris is to be found around waterfront locales across the world; open 24/7 to welcome the foreigner and the stranger. This Catholicism of Western maritime cultures is probably one of the reasons for port cities constantly teetering between both intense devotion and immense disorder.   ·

The Virgin Mary was the deity of the lunar calendar, which reflected tensions between land and sea as well as between opposing cultural systems. The challenge to the calendar came from the landlocked agricultural areas of the globe where the sun represented moral enlightenment, energy and power. Think of how many Sun Kings there have been in history, then think Orange, Orange in France, Orange Free State, Orange County, King William and the Orange Order.

In contrast the lunar calendar started in March and March 25th was Our Lady of Annunciation Day – Lady Day, when the tides turned. The name of Billie Holiday based in New York and singing for the waterfront from the clubs on

52nd Street sang a similar song.

It was the holy days that caused such concern for the Reformation church. People barely worked six months of the year. Lady Day was the start of the great spring tides, which went snaking their way around the globe. This old calendar of women saints is still celebrated by the great carnivals of Latin America, which begin late in February and at Cadiz – in the last month of the old year.

The elimination of holy days helped produce the Protestant Work Ethic. The predominance of forms of casualism on the docks and at sea begs the question whether there was a Catholic anti work ethic – in the sense of spacing work in question to suit a more natural work flow resonant with the tides rather than the clock.

The most vehement assaults of the Reformation Church and State Church were on the cult of the Virgin Mary as by this time she was seen by many within maritime cultures to be the fount of all knowledge. Instead she now became 'the scarlet whore of Babylon'. But her cult had established an undoubted period where there was a feminisation of history, which still remained along the waterfront.

Caravaggio's painting 'The Death of the Virgin' symbolised the death of her cult-hood. It is the dramatic depiction of her removal from society. It is also a parody on the new Church as the shafts of light move left to right; the left or the direction westwards were seen as 'sinister' to the new religious order.

Caravaggio also produced another piece of powerful social commentary in terms of the feminisation of history at a crucial moment with his fresco of Faustina visiting Catherine in prison; lost among the buildings on the left is a full moon. His art signifies the moral bias of the era of female inferiority. Two women enclosed in a prison under a moonlit sky. We are witnessing the great confinement of women, – the new realm of madness caused by the moon – the age of lunacy. The moral cleansing and regeneration of women would now occur with the immersion and ablutive nature of the choking or ducking stool.

Caravaggio died aged 39 years old; he died as he lived in utter disgrace. The rebel, prophet, outlaw. The artist was now a martyr mourned by the rabble and wretched, hooker, homosexuals and holy women alike… His body was found on the shore some way from the harbour of Porto D'Ecole. He was probably looking for a new fugitive night. And he probably would not have wished it to be any other way.

The Reformed Church had succeeded in Europe. The direction of Society was now pure and rational. Rational in that the old triad of cardinal virtues, faith, hope and charity, were being challenged by the least esteemed of all the virtues, Temperancia. She had appeared earlier as mother to invention; clock on her head, bridle in her mouth, spurs on her feet. The human body was now to be bridled and regulated. The virtue of Hope, so long the beacon for the vagabond, the dreamer and the wanderer, was subtly subverted by this new temperance, the dull stalwart of the soul. Caravaggio could never have lived under such circumstance. New words began to appear, 'measure', 'moderation', 'self-control' and 'deferred gratification' in our own post-war age. Caravaggio always ignored self-control and measure. He never recognised any boundary, limit or frontier. He knew that any great art mythology was born out of the melting pot, the hybrid, 'of the mix.'

While England was being 'mapped', the Caravaggisti and the uppity poor of Naples would have to wait nearly 400 hundred years (birth to birth from 1571 to 1960) until the next embodiment of the divine appeared before them. A person like Caravaggio, someone who had eyes all over his body, who could look around him from every angle. The left-footer par excellence whose unpredictability and irregularity made it a sure thing that he too would suffer and who in similar fashion wandered from port city to port city displaying his genius of the move and 'the look' and whose fall came in New York, El Pelusa himself – fluffy hair, tatty head – Diego Maradona.

Look

Someone else who had eyes all over his body, who you knew was looking, 'are you looking at me' at his fingernails, at the wall or even in sleep was Marlon Brando. This sojourn – Waiting for Brando – celebrates the great actor some two years after his death. It also celebrates after him the 50th anniversary of one of his major achievements, the making of the film *On the Waterfront*, and concerns the role of the waterside culture in defining cultural relations in port cities. Liverpool shared with New York as two of these cities the roles of the 'casual workers', dockers and seamen as historic outsiders.

On the Waterfront was based on the 1948 dispute among New York longshoremen (dockers). Some six months earlier the Queen Mary had been held up in New York Harbour by groups of Liverpool seamen protesting about the 'rationalisation' of the casual labour system being imposed upon them in Liverpool. The agreement was intended to regularize working practices through a more intense time-discipline. One writer commented, 'Their illusions of freedom have to be shown to be illusory'. The global waterfront struggles into the 50s and 60s were as much about civil rights and as such fit into the freedom stories of this era.

When the film was produced in 1954 and over the following year of 1954–55, the whole of the Liverpool waterfront was smitten with similar issues of casualism, both within and between unions and the fight for control of working practices, often in opposition to the official union and always within highly localised arrangements. Notwithstanding the efforts of The Seamen's International Union, on the eastern seaboard of the USA, it was the Mob, who many UK seafarers saw as no different to their own union.

For Marlon Brando, part of being an outsider was also the consequence of living in one of the great melting pot cities on the far periphery 'of the nation state'. New York was in America but not of America. It was a city of the 'melting pot' classically defined by sociology with its itinerant populations – sailing from port to port – of Black, Irish, Italian and Jewish seeking to establish free spaces outside of WASP (White Anglo Saxon Protestant) domination. The spaces of freedom created popular culture, as we know it today. A mix of Billie Holiday, Gene Kelly, Frank Sinatra, George Gershwin and Groucho Marx.

The sea, with its movement, links cities as much as it does waterfront labour and cultural practices. Any port city symbolises a way of life, with a push and pull, of an intense localism but also looking out to far horizons. You only have to read the piece taken from the work of Camus which introduces this book about summer in French Algiers to note the way he lovingly describes the freighters in the harbour which he used to swim out to as a kid, and their smells of wood and oil and wine, and for him to imagine the places that they visited and where he would visit in time. A Pier Head Jump in Liverpool meant that you could be having your tea in Bootle or on your way to Argentina.

Seamen and dockers/longshoremen were always the 'outsiders' in terms of work and time discipline and control either by the Mob in New York or the union in Britain. These groups of workers represented an attitude of being against work and time discipline; an energy of being against work whist still having to engage with it. They had realised long ago that their own existence was never to be found in the sole duty of labour. Casualism with its movement 'out' of work was as much a cultural practice as it was industrial.

On the Waterfront hauled to the surface union disputes fought over since 1948 in New York, and 1954/55 in Liverpool. Following two mass dock stoppages in 1954, the year of 1955 saw Rosa Parks refusing to give up her seat and go to the back of the bus, a young group of Liverpool catering stewards on one of the liner boats were also saying 'no' to longer 'more regularised hours'. The disciplining of them caused an overflow of discontent into other areas; most notably the questions of representation by a trade union, which was to many seamen beyond the pale.

Union leaders described the problem as 'a strike by Teddy Boys'. Both the union and ship owners sought to break the strike by sequestering the strikers into the army and threatening to gaol the strikers, which led to the sight of thousands of Liverpool seafarers besieging and scaling the walls of Pentonville prison. The General Secretary of the Seaman's union stated that he was 'philosophically resigned to the fact that Liverpool is full of dissidents'. But just as Martin Luther King Jr. would beseech 'We got to keep the movement moving' – so Liverpool saw the birth of the Seamen's Reform Movement. During this period Paddy Neary, another unknown hero, was sailing on American ships in 1955, which led him to become one of the leaders of the reform movement in 1960 .The 'ripple effect' just like a butterfly opening its wings across the gulf of Mexico teaches us that what seems like an inconsequential action at the time often makes consequential history.

Whilst the film was being made, a couple of Liverpool seamen had jumped ship from the Cunard ship, the Media. They were hanging loose in the bars of Hoboken harbour where the film was being shot. The film crew arrived and told them they would be paid as extras in one of the bar scenes. 'Don't move, just keep drinking and looking straight at the mirror behind the bar, we are just waiting for Brando.' Thus it was that two Liverpool seafarers ended up in one of the definitive films of the 20th century.

To young Liverpool seamen sailing out of a war-torn set of islands, with all its cultural prohibitions and up the Hudson River and tuning in the ships radio to the freedom sounds of jazz, swing be-bop, blues, gospel, New York became their new world. Liverpool and New York, two intense cities whose people are known for their brashness and sense of place.

On the Waterfront took dockside culture, for so long pitied and patronised, from the periphery to the mainstream. Marlon Brando and the look of the method school. Method made it real. He studied acting at the New School in New York, which was a haven for political and cultural refugees from Europe. The greatest influence on him was not Lee Strasburg, but the brassy and sassy Stella Adler, whose acting classes taught young actresses and actors how to become sympathetic observers of human life. She encouraged and stressed habits of emotion and experience, and showed Brando how with that look to get outside of himself. She gave him license to roam. To Stella Adler, the most profound souls would always be found in the depths of society and not in the chivalrous, heroic and noble, which dominated so much of screen cinema. And Stella herself was from a port city, the daughter of émigrés from the Black Sea.

Method acting and its links to realism represented a rejection of the upper-class reserve and staid accents of the British Stage. The Method stood in defiant opposition; emotional, intense and improvised, of the moment. The great director Elia Kazan described American film of the period as the first time 'a view from underneath had been put on the big screen'. These American moving pictures always appealed to moving people and cities on the move.

While attending the New School, Brando lived on W 57th St., at times wracked by insomnia, he haunted the river. What did he see when Liverpool liners docked five blocks away, and anything up to 2000 Liverpool seamen flooded down W 52nd St., – heading towards the diners, clubs and bars of their capital city of the modern world.

In his role as Stanley Kowalski, in A Streetcar Named Desire, he had changed the face of American fashion, wearing fitted blue jeans, the work garb of port workers of New Orleans. Only Brando could have uttered the never to be forgotten shriek of a little boy lost, a cry which brings his wife back into his arms – a cry of 'Stella'. It could have been for his wife, his surrogate mother, Stella Adler, or a great cry for the Stella Maris, the star of the sea. The son, the mother, the sexual being who transgresses roles, the inexpressible tenderness of the glove scene with Eve Marie Sainte demonstrating the cat-like femininity of the port city.

Brando's smouldering incoherence that he brought to the role of Terry Molloy in Waterfront changed again the concept of movie acting. It is impossible to not to be drawn into his emotional intensity where he finishes with his famous 'I coulda bin somebody… I coulda bin a contender… It was you Charlie…' as he blames his brother for betraying him. Potent in the sense that Port cities were often riven by senses of betrayal either by their family or by their 'national' cultures it was part of the intense devotion and chronic disorder which has come to characterise them. Liverpool was known in communist party terms as 'an organisers graveyard', yet few could deny the 'amount of feeling that was always there', particularly when it concerned justice.

These cities have always had millions of contenders, leading day-to-day casual existences, but always somewhere there was the prize; the lucky break, the hopeless hope. In the city of Valencia the patron saint of the port is Our Lady of Hopelessness. At the same time they allow you to dream; they are both cities of the imagination and hope. It is why ships and docks and waterfront areas produce an inordinate amount of singers, dancers, writers, boxers, poets, and civil rights and union activists.

Compare Brando, 'I coulda bin a contender' with a young Liverpool seamen Ritchie Barton writing for Jazz News, filing reports from New York on 'this new sound from Ray Charles called soul jazz'; or another seamen Vinnie McCardle being asked by Lena Horn to open her show in New Jersey. Where else but a port city would produce the actor as a docker/boxer and the seaman as a musical journalist/jazz singer?

For Liverpool seamen, the cosmopolitanism of ideas,

music and other forms of self-expression were always inter-
preted in the random moments of their lives. Playing
instruments, singing and dancing and always performing in
what was a seagoing city, full of self-expression, hopelessness
and full of feisty spirit. And whilst they were all working class,
the word proletarian hardly suits nor adequately defines
them. Just as the 'Method' had been born in New York – so
loud guitars were later to define the Merseybeat generation
and those that followed, rock from Kirby, soul from Bootle,
pop from the city centre.

Four decades later the cross currents of cultural history
were ever present in the stance of Liverpool Dockers, with
port cities supporting their fight in the historic lock-out of
1995–1998, some forty years after *On the Waterfront* made it to
the big screen in New York. This was the final demise of the
maritime economy where the dockers were the carriers
of a city's culture in resisting time impositions.

Liverpool had again found itself isolated within
its own nation state. An international city in terms of its
own people. Its oldest trades seamen and dockers as much a
part of the fabric of the city as the Atlantic skies or the similar populations of Naples, Marseilles, Buenos Aires,
Hamburg or Pernambuco.

The international appeals responded to by port workers,
worldwide, in their support of the lockout reflected an international dimension of waterfront life often at odds with

dominant national culture, where support was less visible.

For engaging in this show of solidarity, the cities that supported the Liverpool dockers were printed on a commemorative tee-shirt. The many listed were equally proud holders of the international tradition, the New Yorks, Sydneys, Odessas of this world, the latter once twinned with Liverpool, Corinto in Nicaragua, Muroroa and Kobe in Japan. These are all global cities often exempt from their own national cultures and still further from the singularity of post-modernism.

As Brando showed there were and still are millions of contenders in port cities despite the demise of the mass maritime economy. While New York still supplies the cornerstone of the 'Method' in terms of acting and observing life in the melting pot, Liverpool still supplies the beats, the rhythms and pulses, and other codas of the musical 'mix' making it one of the party cities of Europe as well as the popular music centre of the world.

We can acknowledge Marlon then as part of this history; like his jeans he could have fitted well in Marseilles, Naples or Algiers. We salute the making of *On The Waterfront* as it passes its fiftieth anniversary, for bringing to a mass audience the seeds of casualised dissent, still dominating port cities and cultures long after the ships have gone. Port cities are a state of mind. Others can think what they like.

Play

Port cities breed abrasive characters, never more abrasive than when they are playing. It is the angry humour of casualism that provides the legacy, so Happy Birthday John Lennon, Lennon of the dissident note. Whenever the lived experience of sea port time is identified it illustrates modes and traditions of casual employment. The cultural history of port cities always reflects the tensions and emotions between home and distance; roots and routes; and what each mean in the hybrid spaces between place, class and love.

Within this environment Lennon and the other Beatles explored how new designs for living in the everyday and in the every night of the 20th century could be remodelled. On the aftermath of his 65th birthday (October 9th 1940) and a quarter of a century since his brutal death on Dec 8th 1980, he would be happy to know that Liverpool still excites with hybrid rhythms and beats – and despite the demise of a maritime economy, other illicit services are always on offer as seasonal as any of the historic wine and grain trades.

The Beatles were the maritime poets of the 1960s, in that they wrote most of their own work; all from a city where a storytelling tradition had always strongly dominated.

Lennon wasn't the first and won't be the last Liverpool fella to be killed in the Big Apple. Plenty had died there before; but they were generally seamen; and no one writes much about them except for a few lines about how they met their end near the waterfront.

John Lennon was, like any ship, a classic rocker and a roller; from a city of comers and goers and with an old man who was a classic restless vagabond from the vast ranks of casual labour from which Liverpool has produced such an array of performers.

Jean Paul Sartre might have been dismissive of 1960s 'yeh-yeh' culture when he said, 'Why does it always finish at 2am? Why don't they continue till later?' He should have known better as one of his favourite cellar clubs of Paris, La Huchette, was originally opened and supported by the same denizens of the demimonde of the waterside communities of the Seine before becoming the model for the Cavern Club in Liverpool.

The bars where the Beatles played in Saint Pauli, Hamburg were similarly the repositories of seamen and dockers; an in between irregular world where day follows night and not vice-versa. The wide appeal of their music lay in its roots and routes. It wasn't just new and accessible; it was local and cosmopolitan; it never stayed within rigid lines; it exploded them and then returned, far beyond Germany and the USA, cyclical as the weather and as irregular as the Liverpool tide.

New sounds and musical movements of dissent and discord were nothing new to Liverpool. The irregular syncopated rhythms of James Reece and the Hellcat Boys, to Duke Ellington, to Johnny Ray and Hank Williams all were taken by the city of Liverpool as being 'their own'. All these artists brought new expressions to musical interpretations of the 'popular'. And these disparate 'sounds' resounding in every area of Liverpool night/day life would become fused, mixed and moulded as Liverpool became a host not just to rhythms of the sea but to new rhythms of life and it continues to this day, 'It is easy to explain yourself in Liverpool as being in a group and on the dole' noted a recent article in the Echo.

Port cities are the amalgams of differing crosscurrents of music, entertainment and self-expression but more importantly with their own ideas of time and movement. Seafaring traditions below decks had always been defined through an oral tradition of storytelling, of itself a major example of seafarer creative expression. Having to deal with constant movement the inhabitants of this intense locale and far horizon, this working class, were always more than their job roles.

When interviewing the Liverpool filmmaker Terence Davies on the South Bank Show in February 1994, Melvyn Bragg's opening lines were 'In no other city is art so closely linked to life'. Why? Because the city, like its people, always makes you to want to sing, dance, perform or write; an amalgam of talents, of feisty spirit; maybe of the hopeless hope, but it's a city of the imagination which allows people to dream. Even today Liverpool football club songs number the largest in Britain. They echo the same cross-currents. 'We'll support you ever more' from Welsh Methodism; 'Scouser Tommy' and 'The Team that You All Know' from the Orange Lodge; 'When The Saints' from Louis Armstrong's New Orleans; 'Yellow Submarine' of the Beatles: Bob Dylan's 'The Mighty Quinn'; 'The Fields of Athenry', a Glasgow song originally of Irish Emigration; and finally the Jewish adaptation of an American Black spiritual and later civil rights anthem 'You'll Never Walk Alone'.

What differentiated John Lennon and the Beatles in general, was not only that they wrote their own music out of this raging city, but they also paid their respects and rhythmic debts to black music genres that had inspired them. This was a powerful feature of support they received from black communities of America. On their first trip to the States, their desire was not to go and meet the presidents and politicians but rather to visit Motown in Detroit, Stax in Memphis and then to meet the greatest mover of them all, the world heavyweight champion, Muhammad Ali.

Julian Bond, the Black Civil Rights leader; author, and educator wrote of his fascination with these four Liverpool white boys when listening to their press conference and hearing them speak of their musical heroes, all of whom were black. It has tended to be forgotten the levels of vitriol they received from the Ku Klux Klan and the White Citizens Council, so much so that their cherished ideal of recording their ground breaking album, Revolver, at the melting pot studios of Stax studios in Muscle Shoals Memphis had to be cancelled. The arrangements made at this river city were scrapped due to the fact that their personal safety could not be guaranteed. The threats had come from the White Citizens Council, terrified of their double crossover sounds impacting on the ears of the pure white culture.

Unreconstructed it was also to awaken latent fears in the mind of Richard Nixon with the case of John Lennon. If music and popular culture in Liverpool had always arisen out of the discordant and dissenting note, rising in tandem is always the politician's eyes and ears of surveillance when musicians and dramatists looked to the 'political'.

But Lennon was from a city which since its birth had always come under the 'gaze' of its own nation state; for centuries an uneasy relationship of both antagonism and compromise. Normally at one and the same time and so often fissured by dissent.

When John Lennon broke away from the Beatles, he was going on another journey. He had always dreamed of sailing the Atlantic; he loved New York where he had the ocean at his back. The docks and the people reminded him of Liverpool, he kept repeating to anyone who would listen during the lost years.

Whether John Lennon was beginning to relive the family tensions of those who go away and those who stay we will never know. Within himself did he reflect the tensions and emotions between home and distance and what that meant in the hybrid dance of place, class, love and sexuality: one of the reasons why the American singer Johnny Ray was so popular in Liverpool?

Freddie Lennon, John's old man was a typical Liverpool seafaring musician. A banjo and song and dance man, who always did a tap-dance, a turn like thousands of Liverpool seamen in Jack Dempsey's bar in lower Manhattan. We can only speculate that Freddie would have played in the famous Liverpool liner 'fu-fu bands'. The name reflecting the old multi-racial mix of the ship's catering crew as the name derives from the Ki Kongan 'fuki' then evolved into 'funky'; and as the old term for people from Liverpool 'scouse' was a stew prepared by African cooks – the rhythms of a Liverpool ship were literally a 'funky soul stew'.

Julia Lennon, John's mum, was also a musician in her own right. And maybe the time her husband was away allowed Julia the chance to make time to make music; a desire for a life of creativity and not conformity. Port cities may have a male domination but they are always female centred. The all girl bands of the sixties especially the Shirelles and the Ronettes hugely influenced the early Beatles, and the

Mersey Sound in general.

And just like Marlon Brando, John Lennon would later suffer the push and pull of mother and son torment. And just like Brando, he lived in one of the blocks leading to the great Westside piers. As though it was another phase of his movement, following a well-worn path trodden by seamen only five streets away where his Dad and other Cunard Yanks would tie up the ship and then flood ashore to the bars and clubs. It was the difference between these few blocks that defined his life.

So for John Lennon, wherever he moved and roamed, it was the ocean, the river, the bay and the sea which gave him a sense of home whilst being away. The distinctive language, the accent of a port city is also markedly different in Naples, New York and Liverpool. Please remember Liverpool is not England, New York is not America and as Maradonna noted in 1990, 'Napoli non e Italia'. John would be pleased to note that the 'nasal' Liverpool drawl he was renowned for, far from becoming converged with an accentless estuary form of English, is becoming instead even more pacey, pronounced and abrasive.

He had to go to the States just as many seamen had done in their different way and so many from Liverpool had done before and since. The waterfront is not such a different place and is still the source of Liverpool's strength in more ways than one. Whether he would have come back to Liverpool is no matter now, and his death still brings sadness to us all a quarter of a century later.

The 1950s and 1960s laid out a 'Rhythm of Dissent'. Girls and boys picking up guitars and turning up the volume. It was about making time to make music by the least assimilated of working class youth – and like any cultural revolution, making music will always be an oppositional stance, especially to time and work discipline. In *I'm Only Sleeping*, off the Revolver album; John Lennon celebrates the right to laze; and the right to prefer the dead-beat of time.

He would have understood completely the Liverpool of the Eighties. The City Council taking on the government and the State whilst at the same time young Liverpool kids are showing their preference for Lennon rather than Lenin, rejecting a culture of labour for one of the raver and embracing a newer kind of 'State'; this one being the club on Dale Street.

Lines taken from *Working Class Hero* suggest, 'You have to embrace time and catch the moments as they fly'. 'What time will do if not seized, what it will destroy if not used; what possibilities it will distinguish if it is not dreamed.' Liverpool is still raging and roaring. Walk down any of the streets of the city; the swaggering gait of young kids, guitar cases over the arm or DJ box in the hand; all suffering for their art and trying to create rather than conform. A journalist recently captured the moment of his own development:

'Even when the local economy was on the brink of ruin and the local council on the cusp of madness, Liverpool continued to produce musicians and writers as if at the epicentre of a creative boom.'

Lennon would have liked it, just as Maradonna loved the spirit of the Scouser, 'all what we are about' in the celebrations following 2005. And as he invoked his own port city football mad dockside of Boca, we think of Brando half a century earlier wandering dishevelled among the thousands of Cunard yanks in their mohair suits on West 52nd Street. Port Cities have the tradition of embracing – not necessarily loving – the outsider, the stranger in their midst as much as they roar out their own defiance.

Freddie, John and Julia Lennon exemplify the conflict penetrating families of those who go away; shaped by sadness and bitterness as waves never return to their source. The confict made sharper from the eternity of casual time where hopes, nostalgia and reminiscence and stories of the future become as mixed as the waters of other times and place… shifting endlessly as the tides which carry them down river and out to sea. Happy Birthday John Lennon, you'd still like it here.

Monday

FUNK-FUN-ON-A-MON the rhythms of the city have
been constant across time – a city of the day and of the
night. The image of the city as one of leisure and pleasure is
nothing new; today, the gravitational pull of Liverpool's rep-
utation as a party city is no different than centuries ago. The
moon is still the mirror of time.

Liverpool really did suffer for its sins during the English
Civil War. The only port which refused to support the
Crown, it fell under Puritan rule which it opposed as well,
even in those days showing a healthy scepticism to authority
in whatever form.

The core value of the Puritan was the fear of movement;
the individual body was seen not as a pleasure zone but a
zone to be measured and controlled. As well as the fact that
Liverpool was full of 'foreigners' – 'strangers' Italian, French
and Spanish; the city had to be purged of the unpure.
Liverpool women were in the forefront of this resistance to
Puritan rule. They became the first 'refuseniks'; documented
as such by refusing to attend the new church on the Sabbath.
Instead they sang and danced (without any help from the

May-pole brigade either).

Their singing and dancing would overflow in what was always a woman's day, Moonday, (Mon-day). – In much of international patois, Mna, Mon, Mona, means female. The Mna-Subail of Ireland were described by a chronicler of the Tudor government as 'going women; moving from country to country sowing sedition'.

As such it was that women's day evolved into 'Merrie Mondays'; even under the dark and dire Puritan rule, Liverpool partied from Friday through till Tuesday morning. Does time past still have a feel of time being present?

In the Victorian era, the 'depraved and promiscuous' nature of the city brought complaints to the British government from various foreign consulates. Such was the allure that whenever a foreign ship docked, it was impossible to keep the crew from going ashore. A lot of them never returned. Besides losing the whole crew, another complaint from the consulates was that it was impossible for the captain to exert his authority. More often than not he was the first down the ladder; men of sober and moral character ruined by a sinful city.

Any crew who dared venture back to ship, would be 'skinned'; a practice of Liverpool prostitutes to rob the seafarers clothes and throw them out onto the street naked, where they would then be chased back to the ship by a mob pelting them with mud. Here was the originator of

Maggie May.

In 1919 Merrie Monday produced what scientists now call symmetry. In the case of Liverpool it was perfect symmetry. The police had gone on strike. The tobacco warehouses were the first to be plundered followed a short time later by the whiskey warehouse. The observer who was describing the scenes, became even more appalled as the night was coming to an end, when a piano was dragged out of a shop on London Road. The observer records that he believes he is in the middle of Dante's Inferno as a 'female demon piano player started beating out the latest rag-time hits being egged on by dancing, prancing drunken figures, all beating perfect time with mugs, bottles and spoons.' The journalist Nancy Banks Smith's first visit to the city was also on a Monday during the second war. She found people desperately scrabbling among the debris by the Rotunda. Her mother feared for the dead. They found out later that Boodles the jewellers had been hit by a bomb. A city of funk – fun-on-a-Mon to the present day funk phenomenon.

Another Monday evening, more than sixty years later, the 79 bus to Netherley. The bus passes three houses, in one window a cross of Saint George, in the next, a portrait of the new Pope, the third one, a poster 'Free Michael Shields'. Two strangers to Liverpool; one from the Bronx; the other from Bilbao. Both here to study and being helped out and being shown where their new digs are. The bus goes through the

South End of the city, chocka block with every different nationality; the world on one bus. Two old fellas, bevvied, are helping the students; both of them ex-seafarers, they live in Seaforth in the high North End, miles away. They're singing 'Strangers in the Night'.

They break into, 'I wanna be around' the bus cracks up. The lad from Bilbao looks around him and smiles. A smile that would light a room. This is his new temporary home. A place on the Mersey instead of the river Nervion. The city's place (identity) on the Atlantic Ocean and the west coast of Europe is still defined by its river and its tides. Liverpool, a city that still moves and is moved by feelings, 'dangerously sentimental or sentimentally dangerous'. A classic city on the edge, Monday night a quarter to eight.

No wave returns to its exact spot. Travelling thousands of miles they reach us and then patiently set off again for the unknown, one by one. A long voyage with only the far horizon for company. And from the intense locale Luis Borges noted, 'My physical body may be in Lucerne, in Colorado or in Cairo, but each morning when I awake, I invariably emerge from a dream, which takes place in Buenos Aires. Whether the dream images involve sierras, or swamps with stilt huts, spiral staircases sunk in cellars, all of them are a particular cross street in the Palermo or Sur quarter. When I am sleepless I am always at the centre of a vague luminous haze, grey or blue in hue… irreparably, incomprehensibly, a porteño, a native-born descendant of the people of the port.'

The inhabitants of Boca Docks, Argentina, those who Tommy Moore would know so well still call themselves 'porteños'. They are the dark-skinned poor who inhabit the lordly southern city of Buenos Aires. This poem was written about them years ago:

'Boca, where the fugitive night returns across nocturnal waters, and where the moon is still the mirror of time'.

EPILOGUE

If you follow and map the old Liverpool dock road, north to south and back and around, the contours and outline take on an image of a huge liner; one which is eternally docked and going nowhere, yet still a permanent reminder of Liverpool's social shape of time and place.

Even though the river's edge lies dormant, the ever-present strength of the seas rhythms still creates differing measures of time and behaviour patterns for those who live within its compass. The daily pulse of the tides will continue to motivate a desire for new planes of experience i.e., movement, in whatever its form.

The paradoxes and contradictions of the waterfront continue to reflect the tensions of routes and roots; home and flight. They also crystallize more than ever the differences of an ever changing world; the plight of being caught between past and present; between city and sea; day and night; black and white, young and old, gay and straight… even between dance and listener based musics. In fact tensions between all difference. Yet port cities are city-worlds where the key to life is integration into the mix, not the celebration of separation.

The people, streets, and the city are still against the rivers' edge; looking out to, across, and sometimes against the world. The further you go inland, the world of steelworks, mines and shipyards were always contained within a much tighter frame of time and place… hence their problems with trying to cope with a post-industrial world. Port cities understand, better than most, change, flux and unpredictability. It was what they were built on.

Yet the silence of the waterfront can allow for the experience not of an old nostalgic disconnection but for a new reconnection. The historical genesis of casualism means that everyday life is subject to the rhythms of scepticism to authority, and time-work discipline.

In Liverpool today, so much employment just seems to be another 'call centre' of a casualised world, yet the swaggering gait of young people, so reminiscent of the old seafarer western ocean roll, becomes even more pronounced when they tell a boss to 'fuck off', or 'shove your job', and leave; exactly the same as the seafaring tradition of desertion; with mobility off and out of the job defining an attitude where angry humour sits alongside laughter and menace. In many employment areas Liverpool today has to recruit authority figures, i.e. bosses, from outside; a culture of resentment to both giving and taking orders. It brings to mind memories of bosses of the 1960s brought in from London to try and impose some order and discipline in the car factories. One spoke of his experience, as 'Liverpool is the only place that when a boss cracks the whip the whip will crack him back'.

The difficulty for people trying to conceive and imagine a world of the unlimited has been due to the traps of enlightenment and the power to create illusions of truth. All the 'ism philosophies contain their stepladder theories of history, where we all have to pass through time in order to reach utopia. This is the foundation of the Big Kid. Time is still our master. In reality as we have tried to show, the only time we can revolt against is that of eternity.

When Luis Borges, John Lennon, Marlon Brando, Caravaggio and Albert Camus defined their port cities there was always something of the 'in between' time about them. These were writers who operated from the melting pot – in between, hybrid places – and they weren't always particular about their definition of political terms but justice always figured in there somewhere.

Living in this changing world… a world more and more being understood by what Stephen Hawking calls the theory of chaotic dynamics, is where all time and motion are deemed to be autonomous, irregular and unpredictable. All relevant laws which govern the universe are random… there is no regularity of order. It's like St Augustine said, 'We don't know where we are coming from and we don't know where we're going.' Therefore if the sky is the limit the gravitational pull of unlimited being will bring spliced and fractured lives. This fracturing will require unburdened shoulders… It is the price of the ticket.

'After the rain, the sun would come, and the place would look like it had been swept in swirls and spirals of light down the long streets before it would settle for the evening and leave you with that long glow they experience in New York… Liverpool, the most beautiful of western Atlantic cities. After the docking was finished he went back to the city and sat in his room. He continued each day down the library or over at the docks. Nothing could keep him away… the walls of his room took on a life of their own.'

Being and time is the product of an in between world like the opening lines of Francis Ford Coppola's Apocalypse Now, 'Saigon… shit… I'm still only in Saigon… When I was here I wanted to be there …' But where is there? The voices of the powerless can create their own truth. They are not illusions but our realities… the timelessness of other places, looking out across endless skies.

They are the same skies of any Atlantic Ocean city. Liverpool's underground railway becomes over ground when it rises into the maritime light. Sandhills, with the unique six face tidal clock in Salisbury dock in view but showing different times on each face, then up to the Anthony Gormley figures on Crosby Beach; none of them moving through time but instead, like ourselves, time is moving through them.

They are our dancers of history. The circular seas still carry with them their own times. Time is still the familiar